BIDDULPH GRANGE

Garden

Staffordshire

The National Trust

Biddulph Grange Garden

Biddulph Grange is one of the most exciting survivals of the great age of Victorian gardening. For over twenty years from 1842 trees, shrubs and a wide variety of other plants from all over the world were brought together at Biddulph amid rockwork, topiary, tree-stumps and an extraordinary collection of eccentric garden buildings. The result is a series of spectacularly picturesque effects and varied microclimates, ranging from the exoticism of a Chinese 'willow-pattern' landscape to the damp of a Scottish glen. Indeed the international scope of the garden has been compared with the contemporary Great Exhibition. Biddulph broke new ground in employing natural screens to create this informal group of separate gardens, each with its own distinct character and set of growing conditions. It was also an early example of an approach to gardening that was to include such great twentieth-century gardens as Hidcote in Gloucestershire. But ultimately, Biddulph deserves to be recognised for its own special qualities, which are characteristic of the Victorian age itself – ingenuity and originality, variety and humour, technical innovation and surprise.

China in 1905

Biddulph Grange has been compared with the Great Exhibition of 1851, which brought together the man-made and natural wonders of the world in much the same way. This view of Queen Victoria and Prince Albert visiting the Exhibition's Indian Pavilion was painted by Prosper Lafaye (Victoria & Albert Museum, London)

One of the stone sphinxes that flank the Egypt topiary pyramid

3

Victorian gardening

A Wardian Case, from Nathaniel Ward's *On the Growth of Plants in Closely Glazed Cases* (1852)

By the early nineteenth century garden owners and designers alike were growing tired of the kind of landscape garden made famous by 'Capability' Brown in the previous century. Brown had transformed the great estates of Britain into broad expanses of grass and water among deceptively natural plantations of mainly native trees. Flowers and ornamental shrubs were confined to walled gardens and pleasure grounds, discreetly sited. From the 1800s Humphry Repton campaigned for a more honestly artful use of flowering shrubs and trees chosen from every continent. This theme was developed by J.C. Loudon, who christened it the 'gardenesque style' in 1832. Encouraged by Loudon and new bodies like the Horticultural Society, the great plant hunters of the period were continually discovering exotic new species of trees, shrubs and other plants in North and South America and the Far East. In 1833 Nathaniel Ward invented the Wardian Case, a portable miniature greenhouse, which enabled live plants to be shipped long distances for the first time and dramatically increased the rate of plant introduction, especially from China. These new introductions were successfully propagated by the leading nurserymen George Loddiges and James Veitch for enthusiasts such as the Batemans of Biddulph Grange.

A corner of the spectacular and influential garden at Alton Towers, Staffordshire, built between 1814 and 1827, from J. C. Loudon's *Encyclopaedia of Gardening* (1850 edition). Loudon described it as 'naturally in a high degree romantic with wood, water and rocks, filled with works of the highest degree of art in architecture and gardening'

A Victorian orchid collector at work

The creators of Biddulph Grange Garden

E. W. Cooke

The garden at Biddulph was principally the work of three people, James and Maria Bateman, its owners, and their friend, the marine painter Edward Cooke.

From the age of eight James Bateman (1811–97) was fascinated by orchids, which became 'the master passion of his life'. He established an important collection at nearby Knypersley Hall and from 1837 published *Orchidaceae of Mexico and Guatemala*, which made his reputation as an orchid expert. In 1838 he married Maria Egerton-Warburton, who came from a leading Cheshire family with a tradition of creative gardening; her brother was the creator of the garden at Arley Hall. Maria was unusual for the period in being interested in herbaceous plants such as fuchsias, and was known as 'that distinguished liliophile' for her love of lilies. In 1840 the Batemans moved to Biddulph Grange from Knypersley, extending the existing vicarage in an Italianate style to accommodate their growing family and adding a series of conservatories in which they grew a wide variety of rhododendrons, camellias and ferns. Cut flowers filled the main rooms and orchids were a particular feature of the table decorations.

In 1849 Edward Cooke (1811–80) paid the first of many visits to Biddulph Grange. The son of a distinguished engraver, Cooke was also the son-in-law of the nurseryman George Loddiges, and was passionately interested in both painting and designing gardens – to the extent that two of his houses were christened 'The Ferns'. With Cooke's help the Batemans created the extraordinary garden that is Biddulph Grange.

The Spode plate made to commemorate James Bateman's 21st birthday; the views of Knypersley Hall (centre) and other local features were probably drawn by Bateman

James Bateman, who, with his wife Maria and the marine painter E. W. Cooke, designed the Biddulph garden

Bateman acquired
this orchid, *Oncidium
lanceanum*, in 1834
from Thomas Colley,
who had discovered
it in British Guiana

James Bateman's love affair with orchids began as a student when he was shown this illustration of *Renanthera coccinea*

The making of the garden

The garden was laid out on a 'b'-shaped piece of marshy land to the south-east of the house, the ground sloping away to the south and west. It was an unpromising site, the soil being poor, the climate cool and wet. The formal gardens adjoining the south front of the house are thought to have been planted first. They consisted of a series of parterres enclosed by yew hedges and featured a 'mosaic parterre' laid out with coloured gravel, clipped box and hybrid china roses. Bateman built the Dahlia Walk below the parterres on an east–west axis. It was filled in when Biddulph became a hospital in the 1920s and has now been reinstated after excavation.

The gardens beyond the Dahlia Walk constitute James Bateman's most original achievement. Within a remarkably small area he created what has been called a 'world image' garden, evoking plants from other ages and continents in a series of separate tableaux. Each of these 'rooms' is hidden from the others by yew hedges, rockwork, mounds of earth, and plantations of trees and shrubs, and connected by circuitous paths or underground passageways to produce unforgettable moments of surprise.

Cooke probably designed all the principal architectural features of the garden, sometimes with the help of clay models. He helped to arrange the rockwork in the Glen and the banks of upturned tree-stumps interplanted with woodland species. Bateman himself was responsible for introducing most of the trees, shrubs and plants.

The series of elaborate parterres in front of the house, photographed in 1905

The Dahlia Walk in 1905

A plan of China by the landscape gardener Edward Kemp from the *Gardeners' Chronicle* (1862)

The decline and rescue of the garden

By the late 1860s the cost of maintaining the Biddulph garden was proving beyond James Bateman's resources, and Maria's health was failing. In 1868 he rented Cooke's house and passed Biddulph to his son, who decided to sell it in 1871. After living in London, the Batemans retired to Worthing, where, although they were both in their seventies, they set about creating a new garden. Maria died there in 1895, James two years later.

Biddulph was bought by Robert Heath, a leading Staffordshire industrialist, who maintained the Batemans' garden to a high standard and added further plants, especially hollies. His son made extensive internal alterations to the house only to see it largely destroyed by fire in 1896; it was subsequently rebuilt. In 1923 the house was converted into a hospital, which it has remained until recently. Extensions to the hospital inevitably encroached on the garden, which from the 1960s suffered increasingly from vandalism and understaffing. However, the essential structure of the garden proved remarkably resilient so that, when an appeal was launched in 1986 to save Biddulph, its particular character was still very much apparent. In April 1988 the National Trust acquired the garden and embarked on its most extensive garden restoration project: to return Biddulph to the glory of its Victorian heyday.

The Chinese temple undergoing restoration

Biddulph was destroyed by fire in January 1896. This photograph was taken after the event, with firemen posing for the camera and the flames painted in

China in 1990, before restoration began

The gateway into China

Bringing Biddulph back to life

The first stages of restoring the Biddulph garden were like an archaeological dig; indeed, the National Trust turned to an archaeologist for help. Careful excavation revealed the Dahlia Walk, which had been completely buried beneath tons of topsoil, complete with its elaborately surfaced paths and a comprehensive drainage system.

After detailed research and analysis of the surviving evidence, the major architectural features were gradually repaired or rebuilt, including the Chinese temple and bridge, the Great Wall, and Joss House, the Shelter House and the Cheshire Cottage. Tree stumps were found to replace those that had rotted away in the Stumpery.

Replanting was even more complicated, as no garden can stand still. Again, careful documentation of what remained was the essential starting-point. Many of the Batemans' original plantings which had prospered were by now over-mature and were starving the garden of light. Where trees and shrubs had to be felled, cuttings were taken so that the original stock could be propagated. If the original variety had died out, the Trust looked first for material collected in the wild, in the spirit of James Bateman. The hybrid rhododendrons and yews were pruned back hard to reinvigorate them. Because the garden had been neglected for so long, the trees are all of a somewhat similar age. The Trust is growing on replacements so that eventually a more balanced age range of trees can be restored, offering continuity for the future.

The Dahlia Walk in 1990 after excavation, but before replanting

Restoring China; charcoal drawing by Martin Shortis

The Glen

Recent restoration

Over the ten years since the garden was opened, work has continued apace. The restoration of Egypt posed an interesting problem. The roof of the tunnel needed repairs, and the pyramid of yew had become misshapen and unprunable. Some of the yews forming the surrounding walls had also died. In 1990, small yews were bought and grown on in boxes so that they could be trained into the correct pyramid shape and moved without checking their growth. Once the old yews had been cut down and the tunnel repaired, the now nearly full-grown pyramid was placed on top and has grown on successfully.

Restoring the Wellingtonia Avenue in 1996 was an enormous task. A large number of the original deodar cedars had died, as had the flanking red chestnuts and yew hedging. The decision was taken to restore the whole avenue in one go. All the young plants were sourced from the countries of origin. The Wellingtonia seeds arrived by post (an avenue in an envelope), and all plants were germinated in the nursery at Biddulph.

The final major restoration project was Mrs Bateman's gardens in 1997–8. These four complicated gardens are on James Bateman's top terrace, created in the 1840s and subsequently swept away by him in the late 1860s, when he truncated the Dahlia Walk. His gardens must have been originally on a series of slopes from west to east following broadly the levels of the Dahlia Walk. The creation of the terrace walls and the obliteration of the lower part of the Dahlia Walk to make the three broad grassy terraces meant that there was no archaeological evidence of the original designs. The layout, therefore, is an interpretation of Kemp's descriptions. A faint shadow of the mosaic parterre was found, and this has been re-created accurately with crushed terracotta and yellow 'grog' (a by-product of the pottery industry).

The other gardens follow the style of Bateman's original. The furthest west includes iron rose-stands designed precisely to the specification that Bateman recommended in 1858 in one of his few surviving letters to his brother-in-law, Rowland Egerton Warburton of Arley. Planting in these gardens has a different character for different times of the year, mainly unusual and exotic plants. In the terracotta pots by the end of the central path under the terrace is *Musa cavendishii*, the dwarf banana of which Bateman was very proud. When he was lecturing at the Royal Horticultural Society, he used to hand out bunches of these bananas to the audience.

The Wellingtonia Avenue after replanting

The Mosaic Parterre

Trimming the Dahlia Walk hedges

The Rhododendron Ground looks its best in May and June

Tree-pruning is essential to allow light into the garden

The year in the garden

From early spring, the varied character of Biddulph's gardens-within-a-garden ensure that, whenever you visit, some will be at their most attractive (in *italics*):

January
Seeds ordered for summer bedding, glasshouse cleaned and disenfected, large yews thinned and cut back

February
Dahlias brought in to force shoots, overgrown rhododendrons thinned and reduced, beds mulched and rotten stumps replaced

March
Paths regravelled, beds weeded and tidied, first mow and summer bedding sown, dahlia cuttings taken, conservation cleaning

April
Italian Garden, Glen, China, Arboretum
Wallflower seeds ordered, dahlias and bedding plants potted-on, worn turf replaced, lawn fed and sprayed for weeds, rhododendrons air layered

May
Italian Garden, Rhododendron Ground, China, Verbena Parterre, Cherry Orchard, Lime Avenue and Glen
Wallflower seeds sown and plants removed, summer bedding and verbenas planted, waterlilies thinned out

June
Rhododendron Ground, China, Mrs Bateman's Garden
Dahlias planted and staked, ivy trimmed back, daffodil clumps cleared, beds weeded and tidied

July
Mrs Bateman's Garden, Rose Parterre, China and Bowling Green
Plants in beds and tubs dead-headed, lawns aerated and gravel paths raked again

August
Italian Garden, Verbena Parterre, Dahlia Walk
Tree survey carried out, dahlias tied in, watering as necessary, cuttings taken of tender plants required for next year

September
Italian Garden, Verbena Parterre, Dahlia Walk
Seed of annual plants collected, dahlias for next year evaluated, hedges cut, bulbs for next year ordered, lawns scarified, aerated and overseeded

October
Dahlia Walk, China, Arboretum, Lime Avenue
Spring bedding wallflowers, bulbs planted, dahlias removed when frosted and placed in storage, Egyptian pyramid trimmed

November
Leaf clearing, bare-root trees planted, ferns and herbaceous plants cut down, beds cleaned and tidied

December
Dahlia beds dug, tree work carried out, large hollies trimmed

Key plants

Surviving original plants

Rhododendron batemani, which is named after James Bateman and first flowered at Biddulph in 1863

A moutan peony, which the National Trust plans to reintroduce to China

BOTANICAL NAME	COMMON NAME	INTRODUCED	LOCATION
Araucaria auracana	Monkey puzzle tree	Archibald Menzies, 1795; William Lobb, 1844	Araucaria Parterre, Pinetum
Cedrus deodara	Deodar tree	1831	Wellingtonia Avenue, Pinetum
Sequoiadedron giganteum	Wellingtonia or mammoth tree	1853	Wellington Avenue, Pinetum
Sequoia sempervirens	Californian redwood	Archibald Menzies, 1795; Theodor Hartweg, 1843	Pinetum, Rhododendron Ground
Pseudolarix amabilis	Golden larch	Robert Fortune, 1852	China
Acer palmatum rubrum	Japanese maple	Robert Fortune	China
Cryptomeria japonica var. *sinensis*	Japanese cedar	Sir Edward Hume, 1842	China
Spiraea japonica fortunei		Robert Fortune, 1850	China
Rhododendron	Hardy hybrid rhododendrons	Raised by nurseries	Rhododendron Ground
Ilex aquifolium cvs	Hybrid hollies	Raised by nurseries	throughout garden
Hedera helix varieties	Ivy	native	Lime Avenue
Thelypteris phegopteris	Oak fern	native	Glen

New plantings by the National Trust

BOTANICAL NAME	COMMON NAME	INTRODUCED	LOCATION
Rhododendron falconeri, hodgsonii, ciliatum, thomsonii		Joseph Hooker	Glen
Pinus ayachuite	Mexican white pine	1840	Bowling Green
Narthecium ossifragum	Bog asphodel	native	Glen
Cardiocrinum giganteum	Giant lily		China
Pinus montezuma	Montezuma pine		Glen
Tsuga mertensiana 'Glauca Nana'	Hemlock	Jeffrey, 1851	Pinetum

Cedrus deodara

Acer palmatum

The future

Although the major restoration of the garden has taken place, the garden will continue to evolve within the original fixed design. Once trials of rhododendrons and azaleas have taken place to see their flowering time, the Rainbow at the end of the Lime Avenue will be replanted. This will be the last feature in the Kemp plan to be put back. The principle behind the replanting everywhere is gradually to work back to plants which are either known to have been at Biddulph through Kemp's descriptions or could have been in the garden in 1846–71. The Italian Garden was replanted in the 1960s with modern rhododendrons and will be replanted with azaleas and rhododendrons to a simpler colour scheme, using cuttings from original azalea plants. The same process will apply in the Rhododendron Ground, which will be replanted with more of the hardy hybrids just becoming available in the middle of the nineteenth century. More planting will take place in the Arboretum. China will be replanted to provide the autumn colour described by Kemp. Every ten years, the Araucaria Parterre needs to be replanted with small specimens of the monkey puzzles so admired by James Bateman. All the hedges will have reached their full height by 2005, when they can be cut precisely. By about 2020, the new young deodar cedars in the Wellingtonia Avenue will be ready for felling to allow the Wellingtonias to grow to maturity, returning the avenue to the original scheme of Wellingtonias only.

Further research will doubtless reveal more about rhododendrons and azaleas dating from the mid-nineteenth century. More information will come to light about bedding schemes and varieties, and as the west-facing side of the Dahlia Walk becomes more shaded, more herbaceous material will take the place of sun-loving dahlias, as in the Batemans' day. The overall aim is to increase the range of plants in the garden to rival that achieved in the nineteenth century.

The replanted Wellingtonias will begin to reach maturity in another 30 years

The Trust plans to plant the Rhododendron Ground with more of the original hardy hybrid varieties

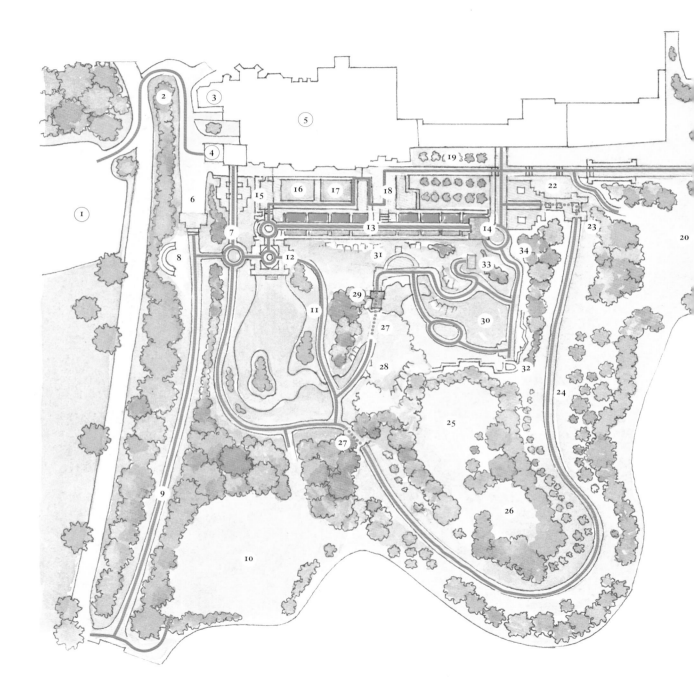

24

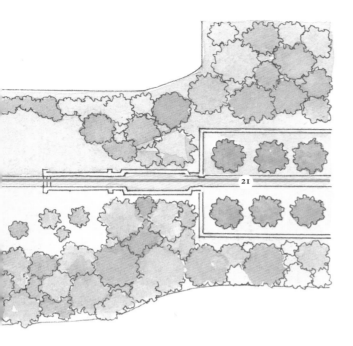

1   Car-park
2   Ice-cream and information
3   Tea-room and toilets
4   Tickets and entrance
5   House
6   Western Terrace
7   Italian Garden
8   Rainbow
9   Lime Avenue
10 Tennis Court Lawn
11 Rhododendron Ground
12 Araucaria Parterre
13 Dahlia Walk
14 Shelter House
15 Mosaic Parterre
16 Mrs Bateman's Garden
17 Lower and Verbena Parterres
18 Rose Parterre
19 Cherry Orchard
20 Arboretum
21 Wellingtonia Avenue
22 Egypt
23 Cheshire Cottage
24 Pinetum
25 Bowling Green
26 Quoit Ground
27 Tunnel
28 Glen
29 Temple
30 China
31 Buffalo
32 Joss House
33 Watch-tower
34 Stumpery

N

The Garden

The following tour provides one way of discovering all Biddulph's attractions, but there is no set route around the garden. Because of the complexity of Biddulph, visitors are advised to consult the map on pages 24 and 25, and the guides who are stationed throughout the garden. Please keep to the paths and bear in mind that at particularly busy times access to some areas may need to be restricted or in one direction only.

The Western Terrace

This terrace looks down over most of the garden, but originally was not connected with it. Entry to the garden is through the west end of the house, which was rebuilt in an idiosyncratic baroque style after the fire of 1896. Beneath the terrace is a small exhibition about the history of Biddulph and its restoration.

The Italian Garden

Italian gardens became popular in Britain in the early nineteenth century. At first such gardens were based quite closely on Italian Renaissance examples, but by the time that the Batemans came to design Biddulph, the label was applied more loosely to any garden with formally arranged flowerbeds, and usually featuring, as here, a stepped terrace and balustrades.

The borders on either side of the paved steps are ribbon planted in typical Victorian fashion with annuals bedded out. Other features are pairs of Irish Junipers (*Juniperus communis occidentale* 'Hibernica'), chosen to emulate Italian Cypresses, and deciduous species of late-flowering *Rhododendron* (azalea). Some of the rhododendrons have been replaced, but others of the original plants have survived, including the white-flowering evergreen *Pieris floribunda*. The central circular stone trough is planted with Golden Yew.

The Italian Garden

A stone seat on the Western Terrace

The Lime Avenue

The Lime Avenue, looking towards the gates designed by E. W. Cooke

The Lime Avenue, which forms the western boundary of the garden, predates the arrival of the Batemans at the Grange. It had been the highway between Biddulph and Congleton, and also served to link the vicarage that had stood on the site of the present house with Biddulph church. The Avenue is now terminated by a fine set of gates, probably designed by Edward Cooke. Beyond was a carriage drive through the former deer-park to the Batemans' other home, Knypersley Hall.

Near the stone seat (also designed by Cooke), Bateman planted a feature he called the Rainbow. Rhododendrons and azaleas that would flower simultaneously were planted in distinct bands of colour on a semicircular bank. Although this feature is now overgrown, the old varieties are being propagated in order to restore it. With equal ingenuity the Batemans aped the shadows cast by the pale green limes by training dark green Irish ivy into scalloped shapes beneath them. Further back, groups of aborescent ivy and common box have been planted to form mound-shaped blocks. Among the wild rhododendrons at the back, there are several plants of the double-flowered hardy hybrid *R.* 'Fastuosum Flore Pleno'.

Those who wish to walk to the end of the Lime Avenue should then follow the path back through the old tennis court area.

The Tennis Court Lawn

This was added by Robert Heath after James Bateman's departure, and is surrounded by banks of azaleas and *Rhododendron* 'Cunningham's White'.

The Rhododendron Ground can be reached through the gap on the north side.

The north end of the Lime Avenue

The Rhododendron Ground

James Bateman was particularly fond of azaleas and rhododendrons, and so decided to plant out the area around the pool with the limited range of species then available and the early hybrids derived from them, together with other plants requiring acid soil. The first such plants came from North America – hence this area's other name, 'the American Garden', although by the 1840s the term was being used more widely to describe a garden in which lime-hating plants from all over the world were grown. The rhododendrons here now are mostly hybrids between hardy North American species and *Rhododendron ponticum* from Turkey and Iran.

The Rhododendron Ground contains the first of the dramatic rockwork in the garden. Massive pieces of Chatsworth gritstone were brought down from the quarry at nearby Troughstone Hill and carefully arranged to suggest that they were naturally formed outcrops. Wild bilberries and heather were also gathered from the moor, and Weeping Holly planted amid the rocks to complete the effect. The island in the centre of the pool is planted with Kilmarnock Weeping Willows.

Follow the path back towards the house, turning right at the raised circular bed onto the Araucaria Parterre.

One of Bateman's more eccentric novelties was the 'upside-down tree', which he replanted with its roots in the air between the Rhododendron Ground and the Lime Avenue. It has recently been reinstated, with ivy and parsley-leaved bramble planted to scramble over the feature

The Rhododendron Ground in autumn, showing the many large clumps of Royal Fern (*Osmunda regalis*) that grow at the water's edge

Rhododendrons were planted at Biddulph by both James Bateman and Robert Heath

The Araucaria Parterre

The four compartments each contain a Monkey Puzzle Tree (*Araucaria araucana*). This was one of the first parts of the garden to be created, and James Bateman later decided to remove it, possibly transplanting the trees to the Pinetum; it was rediscovered after a detailed excavation. Early plans show a centrepiece, but the urn now here was probably meant to stand to the east of the house.

The Dahlia Walk

Bateman shared the Victorians' 'dahlia mania' for these bold bedding plants, carving out a generous sunken walk for them through the middle of his garden. Yew hedges divided the terraced beds into a series of compartments in which the strong colours of the dahlia blooms could be shown off to great effect. The Dahlia Walk was later filled in and only rediscovered after excavations in 1988. The beds have been replanted with dahlias similar to the now extinct cultivars available at the time, together with earlier-flowering herbaceous plants such as phlox, doronicum and hemerocallis, and an edging of lungworts and violas. The Shelter House, which terminates the Dahlia Walk, has been reconstructed from old photographs and archaeological evidence.

The Shelter House in 1905

Two views of the Dahlia Walk in flower. The blooms are usually at their best in late summer and autumn

33

The Lower, Rose and Verbena Parterres

These three parterres, which are thought to be among the earliest parts of the garden to have been laid out, were discovered during the 1988 archaeological dig. The stone walls have been rebuilt on their original foundations and the yew hedges replanted. These will, in time, enclose each level, creating a series of room-like gardens.

The Lower Parterre has been planted up with paeonies and has an edging of *Iris pallida*. On the next level, china roses – including standards and the green-flowered *Rosa chinensis* 'Viridiflora', *R.* 'Hermosa' and *R.* 'Louis XIV' – fill the Rose Parterre. Rectangular beds of verbenas form the central feature of the Verbena Parterre.

The Cherry Orchard

Double morello cherries and other fruit trees are planted here in rows on raised mounds, and pruned uniformly, with *Cotoneaster microphyllus* clipped into bell shapes below.

Beside the path leading from the East Terrace to the Wellingtonia Avenue, Bateman placed pairs of posts connected by chains, up which grew *Clematis flammula* and *C.* 'Miss Bateman'.

The Wellingtonia Avenue

The Avenue was the last and grandest feature that James Bateman added to his garden. It was conceived as a formal set-piece, in which the Wellingtonia (*Sequoiadendron giganteum*) was to dominate. Explorers' accounts of this colossal American tree had aroused great excitement in Europe, and Bateman was among the first to acquire young plants soon after its introduction to Britain in 1853. He planted them alternately with Deodar Cedars which he intended should be removed within twenty years. Unfortunately, Bateman moved away from Biddulph before he was able to complete his plans; his successor, Robert Heath, felled the Wellingtonias instead. After years of decline, the remaining trees were felled in 1995, and the whole Avenue replanted to the original design in the spring of 1996. On the embanked terraces two further ranks of trees are replanted: the Red Chestnuts at the top of the bank set against a dark backdrop of Austrian Pines will complete Bateman's multi-layered scheme.

Retrace your steps to the East Terrace to find Egypt.

The Arboretum. The clearing, which straddles the path to the Wellingtonia Avenue, was planted for dramatic autumn colour with a variety of maples, liquidambars, oaks, hollies and thorns, gorse, white-stemmed brambles and *Rubus odoratus*. A feature is the island clump of Red Maples (*Acer rubrum*) from North America. The dense, suckering evergreen that carpets the banks is *Gaultheria shallon*

The Parterres in their heyday

Egypt

Egypt was one of the most original and distinctive of Bateman's creations; it was also intended that it should be among the garden's greatest surprises.

The French invasion of Egypt in 1798 had inspired a revival of interest in ancient Egyptian art and architecture, reflected in a rash of pyramids and obelisks in European gardens. The fashion waned during the Victorian period, but was still capable of producing extraordinary neo-Egyptian structures like the huge Temple Mills of 1842 in Leeds and the Egyptian court at Biddulph.

High hedges of beech and yew concealed a brilliantly theatrical design in which two pairs of stone sphinxes guarded a hidden court with obelisks of clipped yews standing in small, rectagular lawns. Ahead, stepped blocks of clipped, yew, topped with a pyramid, formed a topiary Egyptian temple. The impact of this area was much diminished after the enclosing hedges were removed in the 1930s; it has been restored through a phased programme of replanting.

Egypt's topiary pyramid is gradually regaining its intended shape

Egypt

Beneath the topiary pyramid, a stone doorway forms the entrance to a dark passageway. At the far end of this, in an unearthly ruby light, sits the sinister Ape of Thoth. This creature was the attendant of the Egyptian god of Botany, and so made an appropriate adornment for this part of the Batemans' 'world' garden. The idea may have been suggested by Cooke, who had drawn Egyptian antiquities in the British Museum and was to buy 'small skeletons, Mexican Idols and Egyptian Gods' at an 1861 auction. Cooke's *Grotesque Animals* (published in 1872) was illustrated with even more bizarre creatures of his imagination, created in response to Charles Darwin's discoveries about evolution, which disturbed both Cooke and Bateman.

The ape was probably sculpted by Waterhouse Hawkins, the creator of the life-size dinosaur sculptures in the Crystal Palace grounds at Sydenham.

The dinosaurs in Sydenham park were created in 1853–4 by Waterhouse Hawkins, who probably also sculpted the Ape of Thoth

(*Right*) The revival of interest in pyramid architecture began in the late eighteenth century with buildings like the 2nd Earl of Buckingham's mausoleum at Blickling in Norfolk

The Ape of Thoth

39

The Cheshire Cottage

The passage from the Ape of Thoth emerges to reveal quite a different scene – the half-timbered Cheshire Cottage. The 'cottage' is really no more than a cleverly conceived façade, the timber frame no more than external battens. The letters 'J & MB' commemorate James and Maria Bateman, '1856' the date of the cottage's construction.

The Pinetum

The stone pine-cones flanking the path outside the Cheshire Cottage announce a new theme: conifers. After orchids, pines were Bateman's great love. The Pinetum was laid out as a showground for one of the richest collections of conifers assembled in mid-Victorian Britain. He took considerable trouble to create a series of irregular mounds which would show off these trees to their best, and gave each of his monkey puzzles an individual nickname.

A tall, multi-stemmed Coastal Redwood (*Sequoia sempervirens*) towers over the Cheshire Cottage, while a fine Wellingtonia grows further along the Pinetum. Other important specimens include *Tsuga mertensiana* (by the entrance to the Bowling Green), *Tsuga canadensis*, cedars and cryptomerias. A group of Swamp Cyprus (*Taxodium distichum*) stands by an unusual variegated oak, its graft union still clearly visible. The medium-height planting consists mainly of holly and golden yew; low sweeps of heather, *Cornus canadensis* and gaultherias carpet the banks.

A glade opens up on the right.

The Bowling Green and Quoit Ground

These two informal lawns, used for many years as a garden dump, have been completely restored. They are planted with a collection of tender, larger-needled South American pines underplanted with evergreens, shrubs and rose species.

Returning to the Pinetum, go through the tunnel to the right into the Rhododendron Ground.

The Pinetum

The Glen

Having drawn rock formations in Scotland, Edward Cooke combined his artistic and practical landscaping talents to supervise the creation of this outstanding piece of naturalistic rockwork.

At first it was planted up with Sikkim and Bhutan rhododendrons which were new to cultivation. Bateman made great efforts to provide ideal growing conditions, but the results were disappointing, and he dispatched the plants to the shelter of his conservatory. Many of these species have recently been reintroduced here in the hope that the maturity of the surrounding planting will offer them greater protection.

Bateman and Cooke shared an enthusiasm for ferns, planting some 22 different species and cultivars here, together with a collection of semi-aquatic plants such as *Pinguicula* and perennials like the New Zealand Flax (*Phormium*) and pampas grass.

The opening in the rock ahead leads through a tunnel into China.

Rhododendrons grow between the rockwork that leads to the Glen

China

This is perhaps the most memorable part of Biddulph and the most famous of its 'national' gardens. Completely hidden from the rest of the garden by high banks, trees and walls, it evokes a magical Victorian vision of China. As one emerges from the darkness of the tunnel, a Chinese willow-pattern plate comes to life before one's eyes. A zig-zagging fence leads the path to an ornate wooden bridge over a pool beside a temple and surrounded by ornamental trees.

This elaborately theatrical setting was created to display many of the exotic plants that were being brought back from the Far East, especially those discovered by the plant hunter Robert Fortune: *Pseudolarix amabilis*, *Spiraea japonica fortunei*, *Piptanthus nepalensis* and *Paulownia imperialis*. Other particular features are the purple-leaved Japanese Maples (*Acer palmatum*), *Cryptomeria japonica*, hostas and Tree Paeonies planted amid tufa, a rock brought from Derbyshire and more often found in the grottoes of eighteenth-century gardens.

One of the massive stone gateways leading into China

The wooden footbridge in China

The view from the Chinese temple

The stone frog

The path through China leads past a gigantic frog sitting on the wall, then under a great stone Chinese gateway into a semicircular space dominated by Waterhouse Hawkins's extraordinary sculpture of a Chinese idol in the form of gilded water buffalo. Below this beast are two gravel-filled parterres cut out of the turf in the shape of dragons. Continuing the theme, Bateman built a 'Great Wall of China' along the western ridge with the ornamental Joss House perched at one end and a stone watchtower to the north.

The temple, with its adjoining balustraded terrace overlooking the lake, is one of the last examples in Britain of a building in the Chinese taste, a fashion that had been pioneered in the late eighteenth century by Sir William Chambers with his Chinese pagoda at Kew. The temple is richly decorated with gilded dragons, sea horses, carved grebes and hanging bells. The multi-coloured roof tiles, made originally by Minton Hollins, were removed at the turn of the century, and have been replaced, copying fragments discovered in the pool. The building's striking colours are a faithful recreation of the original, although they bear very little relation to those of an authentic Chinese garden temple.

The path winds out of China through the Stumpery.

The Stumpery. Stumpwork was one of the most unusual features of Victorian gardening. Tree roots and stumps were carefully excavated and then set upside down into banks of earth to form a decorative framework, around and over which ivies and other trailing plants could be trained

The dragon parterre

The Chinese temple from across the pool